# NEW CANADIAN KID & INVISIBLE KIDS

# ALSO BY DENNIS FOON

## PLAYS

*Chasing the Money*
*Kindness*
*Mirror Game*
*Rick: The Rick Hansen Story*
*Seesaw*
*Skin & Liars*
*War*

## NOVELS

*Double or Nothing*
*Skud*

The Longlight Legacy
*The Dirt Eaters*
*Freewalker*
*The Keeper's Shadow*

for more information visit www.dennisfoon.com

# NEW CANADIAN
# & KID
# INVISIBLE KIDS

## BY DENNIS FOON

PLAYWRIGHTS CANADA PRESS
TORONTO

For professional or amateur production rights, please contact:
Michael Petrasek, Kensington Literary Representation
34 St. Andrew Street, Toronto, ON M5T 1K6
416.848.9648, kensingtonlit@rogers.com

Library and Archives Canada Cataloguing in Publication
Foon, Dennis, 1951-
[Plays. Selections]
        New Canadian kid ; & Invisible kids / Dennis Foon. -- Second edition.

A collection of two plays.
Issued in print and electronic formats.
ISBN 978-1-77091-954-9 (softcover).--ISBN 978-1-77091-955-6 (PDF).--
ISBN 978-1-77091-956-3 (EPUB).--ISBN 978-1-77091-957-0 (Kindle)

        I. Foon, Dennis, 1951- . New Canadian kid. II. Foon, Dennis, 1951- .
Invisible kids. III. Title. IV. Title: New Canadian kid ; and, Invisible kids.

PS8561.O62N483 2018          jC812'.54          C2018-904731-3
                                                C2018-904732-1

Playwrights Canada Press acknowledges that we operate on land which, for thousands of years, has been the traditional territories of the Mississaugas of the New Credit, the Huron-Wendat, the Anishinaabe, Métis, and the Haudenosaunee peoples. Today, this meeting place is still home to many Indigenous people from across Turtle Island and we are grateful to have the opportunity to work and play here.

We acknowledge the financial support of the Canada Council for the Arts—which last year invested $153 million to bring the arts to Canadians throughout the country—the Ontario Arts Council (OAC), the Ontario Media Development Corporation, and the Government of Canada for our publishing activities.

 Canada Council   Conseil des arts
for the Arts     du Canada

 ONTARIO ARTS COUNCIL
CONSEIL DES ARTS DE L'ONTARIO
an Ontario government agency
un organisme du gouvernement de l'Ontario

 Canadä

 Ontario
Ontario Media Development
Corporation

*For all immigrants and refugees, everywhere.*

# INTRODUCTION
## BY MARCUS YOUSSEF

For more than twenty-five years, Dennis Foon has been one of
my writing heroes. I first encountered his plays for young people
when I was a student at the National Theatre School in the early
1990s. I was running a summer theatre employment program for
"at-risk" youth ("potential early-school-leavers" was the preferred
jargon of the time). I needed to find plays to help them understand
what a play was. I needed plays that believably represented the lives
of young people with nuance, complexity, and depth. Most of all
I needed to find plays that a group of young people with limited
trust of adults might actually *like*. That's when I found the work of
Dennis Foon.

In my experience, young people almost always love Foon's
plays. I think that's largely because he treats his young characters
as fully formed human beings, each with their own idiosyncratic
and legitimate perspectives. In Foon's work, children and teens are
invariably intelligent, perceptive, angry, contradictory, and joy-
ful—i.e., as multi-dimensional and complicated as the adults who
hover at their stories' peripheries. The conflicts these young people

confront—almost always as the result of adult decisions they have little or no control over—reflect the deep complexity all children deal with as a matter of course in their actual lives. Without ever being preachy or overly precious, Foon's plays treat the often-invisible pain and struggles of the young with a fundamental, unshakable respect. This, along with the generosity of Foon's irrepressible sense of humour, is why they are produced over and over again, in multiple languages, across the globe.

Nowhere is this more clear than in his plays, *New Canadian Kid* and *Invisible Kids*. Of particular note, in this edition Foon offers us an updated version of *Invisible Kids*. He has reworked a story he originally wrote in the mid 1980s to reflect the reality of the world's most recent great migration. This movement of countless innocents from a war without end in Syria and Iraq must be close to the clearest example of the adult world's abject failure to protect its children. In *Invisible Kids*, Ranem is a refugee from Syria, a boy who has recently arrived in what is an utterly recognizable, multi-ethnic, contemporary Canadian schoolyard. Like migrants everywhere, he courageously attempts to join a new group of friends, each of whom also represents a kind of "difference" as defined by the adult world around them. As a much-longed-for school trip is threatened because the rules of this adult world will prevent Ranem from crossing a border, this group of friends comes face to face with a truth many grown-ups have trouble comprehending: not all differences are the same, and each produces its own unique set of consequences.

What unfolds in this fable-like story, as each of the friends attempt to untangle their complex relationships to each other and the baffling rules of the world around them, is a masterwork in storytelling for young people. It is both completely believable and resists saccharine magic solutions. As all young people know, and as both of these plays remind us, in the real world many things do not turn out for the best. At the end of *Invisible Kids*, Ranem is still unable to cross the border, even though the coveted class trip was only made possible because of his achievement as a young scientist. Despite not getting what they want, however, Ranem and his new friends still achieve something remarkable. They take the crucial step that defines both great drama and the essence of authentic community: they take action. That this action doesn't solve the problem they are facing is of secondary importance. What matters, Foon reminds us, is the fact that they do actually try to do something, together. It is an act of collective solidarity that transcends their individual differences and allows this group of individual young people to begin to imagine themselves not as a collection of "me's" but as an "us."

In the original *Invisible Kids* the character of Ranem was named Thiun. He was a refugee from Vietnam. It is a bit shocking how "well" this update works and how utterly believable the change of characters plays. And yet maybe that's not so surprising. Forty years ago, huge numbers of people fled Vietnam in the wake of a brutal, decades-long war led by imperial powers and their regional proxies. Today, huge numbers of people flee the Middle East in the midst of a decades-long war led by imperial powers and their regional proxies. For me, this is a reminder that, while names and geopolitical circumstances change, the devastating consequences of militarism and power do not. There will always be people seeking refuge. And the citizens of countries relatively untouched by these wars will— like the children in these plays—always be faced with a question: how do we choose to treat those people? Do we stand with them and embrace their struggles as our own? Or do we cut ourselves off, mumble homilies about how lucky we are, and turn inward, donning our good fortune like armour, designed to keep the less fortunate out.

These two plays carve out a path for all of us—not just kids—to begin to make the choice.

Marcus Youssef's fifteen or so plays include *Winners and Losers*, *King Arthur's Night*, *A Line in the Sand*, *Ali and Ali and the aXes of Evil*, *Adrift*, and *Jabber*. They have been performed across North America, Europe, and Asia, from Seattle to New York to London, Reykjavik, Hong Kong, and Berlin. Marcus is the recipient of the Siminovitch Prize in Theatre, the Vancouver Mayor's Arts Award, the Rio Tinto Alcan Performing Arts Award, the Floyd S. Chalmers Canadian Play Award, the *Seattle Times* Footlight Award, the Vancouver Critics' Choice Award (three times), and the Canada Council Staunch-Lynton Award.

# NEW CANADIAN KID

*New Canadian Kid* was first produced by Green
Thumb Theatre for Young People in September
1981 on tour in British Columbia, and at the
Calgary International Festival for Young People,
with the following company:

Mother: Kathryn Daniels
Nick: Robin Mossley
Mench: Wendy Noel
Mug: Colin Thomas

Directed by Jane Howard Baker
Set and Costume Design by Sandy Cochrane

## STAGING NOTES

Apart from the opening scene that takes place in Homeland, the entire action of the play occurs in Canada: a school classroom, playground, and the home and porch of Nick's family.

After much experimentation, I have come to the conclusion that, with this play, simplest is best: the set should consist of a freestanding window that represents the home interior. Covered with a blackboard, it serves as a backdrop for the school scenes. Three stools may be used by the kids in the classroom scenes. Mother may use a chair that sits by the window. If you feel extravagant, treat yourself to a Canadian flag that may stand upstage.

The colour of Homeland is green. Nick and his mother should be dressed completely in shades of green, in contemporary store-bought clothing. There is a very important reason for this: the Homelanders should look alien to the Canadians—and to the audience—but their costumes should not be identifiable to any specific country.

The Canadians should be dressed in other primary colours that Nick may later integrate into his costume he becomes more comfortable in Canada, such as when he receives clothing. The audience should identify with them from their first entrance, so their costumes should be very similar to what the audience finds acceptable and appealing.

## PLAYERS

Mother, a woman from Homeland
Nick, her son
Mench, a Canadian girl
Mug, a Canadian boy

Note: Many productions have chosen to shift the characters' genders, with the playwright's wholehearted approval.

## SETTING

The present

## THE GIBBERISH

Because the play is attempting to show the audience what it is like to be in a country without the same language or customs, the Homelanders speak English and the Canadians speak gibberish, a kind of language invented by the actors in each production based on the dialogue I provide.

The original gibberish was created by Colin Thomas and Wendy Noel, and since that first production it has been constantly modified and updated by myself and other actors. So the gibberish in this script has been evolving for thirty-seven years, a necessary process because the gibberish should include local and topical references. Use the gibberish in this text as a launch point, inventing a completely new language if you want.

# A NOTE ON INTERNATIONAL PRODUCTIONS

This play has been produced innumerable times by theatres outside of Canada. For example, in the UK and USA it's retitled as *New Kid*, and in Denmark it is *Rigtig Dansk Dreng*. All productions are urged to localize the gibberish, references, and production elements.

*NICK addresses the audience.*

**NICK:** My name is Nick. I come from a country called Homeland. But now I live in Canada.

**MOTHER:** *(off)* Nick!

**NICK:** Coming . . . The day I left Homeland, I said goodbye to my friends. I told them I'd write, that I'd come back soon.

**MOTHER:** *(off)* Nick!

**NICK:** . . . They gave me this lunch bowl as a going-away present. I like my friends a lot. It was hard to say goodbye.

**MOTHER:** *(entering)* Come on, Nick, you haven't finished packing.

**NICK:** I was saying goodbye to my friends. Look what they gave me.

**MOTHER:** That's beautiful, Nick. We'll have to pack it really carefully. Now come on, Dad's waiting for us.

NICK: Mom, do we have to go?

MOTHER: Nick, we've talked about this already.

NICK: I want to talk about it again.

MOTHER: It's going to be okay. Canada's going to be good for all of us.

NICK: I don't want to leave my friends.

MOTHER: You'll make new ones. Everything's going to be new. Even the language—English.

NICK: English? It'll be like learning to talk all over again.

MOTHER: No, it won't even take a week. You'll love Canada. Let's go.

NICK: Canada. So far away. I'd seen airplanes before but I'd never been in one. I was scared at first, everything was shaking. But then we were up in the sky. I missed a half hour of it though—accidentally I locked myself in the washroom.

When we landed, we were in Canada. It was winter, really cold. My very first day in Canada, I licked some snow from a frozen fence post and my tongue got stuck. Later, after we found a place to live, I started to go to school.

*MENCH, a Canadian girl, enters. She brings her stool downstage. She is listening to her iPhone, dancing to the beat, singing a current pop hit in gibberish. As her outrageous performance peaks, MUG, a Canadian boy, enters. He picks up his stool and places it next to hers. She is too involved in her show to notice him. MUG is amused and mimics her behind her back. Finally he removes an earbud from one of her ears.*

MUG: Lo, Mencha. [Hi, Mench.]

MENCH: Lo, Mog. [Hi, Mug.]

*MUG parodies MENCH's singing and dancing. She chases him. MUG suddenly stops at the blackboard. Written on it are some math problems titled: "Homvorko Matmatiko."*

MUG: Ah, poopit! Es sue kwit vos homvorko? [Oh crud! Did you finish your homework?]

MENCH: Yo. [Yes.]

MUG: Givva may. [Give it to me.]

MENCH: Nax. [No.]

MUG: Aw, moose. [Aw, come on.]

MENCH: Costa. [It'll cost you.]

MUG: Einst queenie coin. [A quarter.]

MENCH: Nax. [No.]

MUG: Doost queenie coin. [Two quarters.]

MENCH: Sue-she. [Okay.]

*She takes the money. MUG starts copying the work from her notebook into his. MENCH nervously watches for the teacher.*

Zapit! [Hurry up!]

MUG: Ee bee! [I am!]

MENCH: Zap zapit! [Move it!]

MUG: Vor shure! [All right!]

*MENCH goes to him:*

MENCH: Givva may. [Give it to me.]

MUG: Nax. [No.]

MENCH: Kwit? [What?]

MUG: Doost queenie coin. [Two quarters.]

MENCH: Ee finko Mastah Tuto. [I'll tell the teacher.]

MUG: Einst queenie coin. [One quarter.]

MENCH: Sue-she. [Okay.]

*MUG takes the money.*

MUG: Audio vos? [Can I listen?]

MENCH: Einst queenie coin. [One quarter.]

MUG: Sue-she. [Okay.]

MENCH: Vo nax cronkit, goobo. [Don't break it, goof.]

MUG: Ee nax cronkit, boofo. [I won't break it, bozo.]

*He listens. Stops.*

Nax da volumo, Mencha. Turnst da ono. [No volume, Mench. Turn it on.]

*MENCH turns the volume up all the way. MUG yowls. She turns it down. He starts to get into the music.*

Ohh yo . . . [Oh yeah . . . ]

*MUG now begins his own performance, in gibberish, to a different popular pop song. As his gyrations peak, NICK enters, carrying his bowl. MUG doesn't see NICK and continues. MENCH does and starts to giggle. Then MUG notices NICK and stops, embarrassed. But then, recovering, he jokes with MENCH, pointing at NICK, who is dressed in the green colours of Homeland.*

Gander chay: Kermit da Froglet! [Look at him: Kermit the Frog!]

**MENCH:** *(to NICK)* Sue vancha rumpabum? Stat. [You want a stool? There.]

*NICK does not understand. MENCH points to a stool.*

Rumpabum! [Stool!]

**MUG & MENCH:** Rumpabum! [Stool!]

*NICK starts to get the idea and goes to the stool. MENCH indicates that it is supposed to be downstage like theirs.*

**MENCH:** Nax. Parkit! [No. Put it there!]

*NICK does and sits.*

Lo. Ee noma Mencha. Kay vo? [Hi. My name is Mench. What's yours?]

*NICK does not reply.*

**MUG:** Chay noma Mencha! Kay vo! [Her name is Mench! What's yours!]

**NICK:** I don't understand.

**MUG:** *(mimicking NICK)* Ah don unnerstan.

*MENCH laughs.*

Sue es Homelander, nax? [You're a Homelander, aren't you?]

**NICK:** Excuse me?

**MUG:** *(slowly)* Homeland.

**NICK:** Oh, yes. I am from Homeland.

**MUG:** *(mimicking NICK)* Ooo yas, I am frum Homeland.

*MUG laughs at his own joke. MENCH joins in. NICK smiles.*

**MENCH:** Ee noma Mencha. Mencha. [My name is Mench. Mench.]

**NICK:** Oh. Your name is Munch. You're Munch.

**MUG:** *(correcting NICK)* Mencha.

**NICK:** Mencha.

**MENCH:** Chay Mog. [His name's Mug.]

**NICK:** Muck.

**MUG:** *(irritated)* Mog!

**NICK:** Mog! . . . My name is Nick.

**MENCH:** Snick.

**NICK:** No, just Nick.

**MENCH:** Just Nick.

NICK: Nick. Nick!

MENCH: Nicknick.

MUG & MENCH: Nicknicknicknicknick!

> *MUG and MENCH stand up and begin singing "O Canada" in gibberish. NICK is bewildered.*

Bo Nadacan
Vo has et terrid bland
Lo parrot bleak
Ein toto voyo sand

> *MENCH notices that NICK is still seated.*

MENCH: Shtanten! [Stand up!]

MUG: Shtanten!

NICK: I'm sorry, I don't speak English yet. Not for another week.

MUG & MENCH: *(singing)* Mik sheeny pumps
Nos gander zam
Oh yoyo maypo tree

MUG: Shtanten, boof! Shtanten—como dis! [Stand up, goof! Stand—like this!]

> *MUG demonstrates.*

**MUG & MENCH:** *(singing)* Bo Nadacan
Nos shtanten gro
Por tee
Bo Nadacan
Nos shtanten gro
Por tee

*At the end of the song NICK stands. MUG and MENCH sit.*

**MUG:** Perfecto! [Perfect!] Ee nama saluto de Maypoleepo. [Now we salute the flag.]

*MUG makes a ridiculous gesture. NICK is skeptical and looks to MENCH, who quickly copies MUG. NICK then decides to follow. MUG now does a strange march around his stool. MENCH copies him. NICK follows. MUG puts his face down on his stool. MENCH does too. NICK shrugs and goes along with it. As soon as NICK has his face down, MUG and MENCH break their pose and sit. They stifle their laughter for a moment, but then it is too much and they crack up. NICK looks, real- izes what has happened, and sits down. MUG and MENCH now begin their homework. MUG takes out his phone to use as a calculator.*

Ay, Mencha, chaka may chello. [Hey, Mench, check out my phone.]

**MENCH:** Kwan sue score it? [Where'd you get it?]

**MUG:** May moom-eye ee pop-eye. [My mom and dad.]

**MENCH:** Marzipan. [Excellent.]

**MUG:** Ver shure. [For sure.]

**NICK:** That's a nice phone.

**MUG:** . . . Homelanders nax hab chellos. [Homelanders don't have phones.]

**MENCH:** Sue jesto. [You're joking.]

**MUG:** Nax jesto. [For sure.] Gander dis, homee! [Look at this, homie!]

*MUG and MENCH go to the blackboard. MENCH reads the math problem and MUG punches it into his phone.*

**MENCH:** Saskatoon moosh rubiks da sublock dim sum: [Sixty divided by forty subtracted by twelve equals:]

**MUG:** Kalamazoo. [Eleven.]

*MENCH checks her notebook against MUG's solution.*

**MENCH:** Nax correcto. Attempto encoro. [Wrong. Try again.] Saskatoon moosh rubiks da sublock dim sum:

**MUG:** Kalamazoo.

**MENCH:** Nax correcto encoro. [Wrong again.]

**NICK:** You're pushing the wrong button.

**MENCH:** Nicknick, sue vancha trot? [Nick, you want to try?]

**NICK:** What?

**MENCH:** *(to MUG)* Al chay trotit. [Let him try it.]

*MUG is appalled at the idea.*

**MUG:** Ein Homelander trot may chello? [Let a Homelander try my phone?]

**MENCH:** Yo. Gopher shtat. [Yeah. Go for it.]

*She gives MUG a poke. He relents.*

**MUG:** Yoyo. [Okay.]

*MUG gives it to MENCH. MENCH hands it to NICK.*

**NICK:** I can try it?

**MUG:** Nax cronkit. [Don't break it.]

**MENCH:** *(to NICK)* Saskatoon moosh rubiks da sublock dim sum:

*NICK finishes the problem quickly as she reads it. He shows her the answer on the phone. She checks.*

. . . Correcto. [Right.]

MUG: Gibba may. [Give it to me.] Ee deeit, gibba may! [I said, give it to me!]

*MUG grabs for the phone, knocking it out of NICK's hand. It falls to the ground. MUG picks it up, checks it.*

Ee be crookee. Ee bee toot a crookee. [It's broken. It's totally broken.]

NICK: I didn't do it on purpose, I . . .

MUG: Chay cronko mein chello. [He broke my phone.]

NICK: I'm sorry, I didn't . . .

MUG: Mootard! [Idiot!]

MENCH: Et mo gander shtat. [Let me see that.]

*She takes the phone, bangs it on a stool.*

MUG: Oy! [Hey!]

MENCH: Bom. Ee bee sue-she nama. [Done. It's fixed now.] Gander. [Look.]

*She hands it to MUG. He checks it and sighs with relief. He then turns angrily to NICK:*

MUG: Sue nax toucha mein chello encoro! [Don't you touch my phone again!]

*The bell rings. MENCH and MUG start to exit.*

MENCH: Nax Nicknick blan. [It wasn't Nick's fault.]

MUG: Homelander blan ver shur. [It was the Homelander's fault for sure.]

*After MUG and MENCH exit, NICK addresses the audience.*

NICK: I didn't break it after all—it was okay. Mencha fixed it. And what a great phone.

*MENCH enters.*

MENCH: Munch mow-er. [Lunchtime.]

NICK: Munch mow-er?

*She points to her mouth and exits.*

Oh, lunchtime, great.

*(to audience)* I keep my lunch in this bowl my friends gave me. In Homeland we say that the bowl keeps food and the food keeps life. I like to think of my friends.

Hey, wait for me!

*NICK runs off. MENCH and MUG enter with their lunches and sit. MUG pulls out a sandwich and grimaces.*

MUG: Gahh. Sardeenos mik wheezechiz. [Sardines with Cheez Whiz.]

*MENCH reveals a Big Mac.*

MENCH: Fridgo grosta mac. [Cold Big Mac.]

*They put their sandwiches back into their lunch boxes in disgust. MUG finds something in his.*

MUG: Wo yoyo! May moom-eye pack ein grosta Hershee. Whacko! [Wicked! My mom packed me a giant Hershey's. Excellent!]

*He's in seventh heaven. He takes a bite of the chocolate and groans ecstatically. MENCH watches him hungrily. MUG notices.*

. . . Sue vanchen chunken, Mencha? [You want a piece, Mench?]

MENCH: Yo! [Yes!]

*She takes a bite.*

Taka. [Thank you.]

*MUG opens the wrapper and sees a gigantic bite in his chocolate.*

MUG: Porko! [Pig!]

*MENCH smiles at him sheepishly. NICK enters. They watch him. He sits.*

Sue tinker chay vanchen chunken? [Do you think he wants a piece?]

MENCH: Ver shur. Gibba Nicknick chunken da hershee. [For sure. Give Nick a piece of chocolate.]

MUG: Nicknick? Nax vay. [Nick? No way.]

MENCH: Oh, moose. [Oh, come on.]

*(to NICK)* Nicknick, sue vantcha chunken da hershee. [Nick, do you want a piece of chocolate?]

NICK: I don't understand.

MUG: Ee bay hershee. Sue nax condo kwit hershee set? [This is chocolate. Don't you know what chocolate is?]

MENCH: Gibba Nicknick bo chunken. [Give Nick a piece.]

MUG: Nax. [No.]

MENCH: Sue gibba mo encora chunken? [Will you give me another piece?]

MUG: Sue-she. [Okay.] Itsee bit. [Just a bit.]

*MENCH takes it.*

MENCH: Ver shur. [For sure.]

*MENCH runs over to NICK with the chocolate.*

MUG: Oy! [Hey!]

MENCH: *(to NICK)* Tastay. [Taste it.]

*NICK takes it cautiously.*

NICK: This looks like chocolate.

MENCH: Tastay. [Taste it.]

*NICK tentatively nibbles on it.*

NICK: It is chocolate. I've never seen chocolate wrapped like this! Thanks a lot.

MENCH: Sue bettersket. [You're welcome.]

NICK: *(to MUG)* Thank you very much, Mug.

*MUG smiles back at NICK, then, taking the candy back from MENCH, wipes off the chocolate where NICK bit it. NICK does not see this because he has taken the lid off his bowl and begins eating from it. MUG puts his candy away, then sniffs the air.*

MUG: Kwesta fumo? [What stinks?]

MENCH: Kumquat fumo? [What stink?]

MUG: Sue nax sniffo da fumo? [You don't smell that stink?]

*MENCH sniffs, then grimaces.*

MENCH: Yo yo. [Oh yeah.]

MUG: Ee bee huey. [I'm sick.]

MENCH: Ee bee spewy. [I'm really sick.]

MUG: Oy, Homelander—sue sniffo da fumo? [Hey, Homelander—you smell that stink?]

NICK: I don't understand.

*MENCH indicates that he should sniff.*

MENCH: Snaffa whifto—ee bee grosta kaka. [Take a whiff—it's really gross.]

NICK: You want me to smell something?

*NICK sniffs.*

I don't smell anything.

MUG: Lowd—ee bee grow dee. Ein fido musta poopit. [Lord—it's horrible. A dog must have pooped.]

*MUG checks his shoes.*

Nax stompen may bootee. Chaw kay vos bootee, Mencha. [There's nothing stuck to my shoes. Check your shoes, Mench.]

*MENCH checks hers. They're clean and she sighs with relief.*

**MENCH:** *(to NICK)* Chaw kay vos bootee, Nicknick.

**NICK:** My shoes?

*He checks: they're clean. He shows them.*

**MENCH:** Nax.

*Meanwhile, MUG has been sniffing all around, attempting to trace the smell. Finally, he leans over NICK's bowl, sniffs, and jerks away.*

**MUG:** Oy, oy! Ee bee chay gorda! Ee bee munch da Nicknick. [Hey, hey! It's his bowl. It's Nick's lunch.]

**MENCH:** Sue jesto. [You're kidding.]

**MUG:** Yo, ver shur. Snifot. [Yes, for sure. Smell it.]

**NICK:** Hey, what's bugging you guys? I'm trying to eat my lunch.

*MENCH sniffs NICK's bowl and gasps.*

**MENCH:** Kay bee shtat, Nicknick? [What is that, Nick?]

**NICK:** Does this smell bother you? It's just a seasoning, like salt. I don't know how you eat food without it.

**MUG:** Ee vanna corpso! [I want to die!]

NICK: You don't have to make those faces. If you tasted it, you'd probably like it.

MUG: Chay vanch may tastay? [Does he want me to taste it?]

MENCH: Goo fo shtat. [Go for it.]

MUG: Sue vanch may tastay? [You want me to try it?]

NICK: Yeah, here. Taste it.

MUG: Nax. [No.]

MENCH: Oo, chargit, nerd noggin. Tastay. [Oh, come on, big mouth. Taste it.]

MUG: *(angrily)* Nax taka, Mencha!! [No thanks, Mench!!]

MENCH: Ooooo. Nicknick, Mog ein igg squirter. [Ooooo. Nick, Mug's a chicken.]

MUG: . . . Sue-she. [All right then.] Skay may doma dis? [How do I do this?]

NICK: Just take a little bit like this.

> *NICK demonstrates, holding a little food with his thumb and index finger.*

See? Just take a little bit in case you don't like it.

*MUG takes a bit in his fingers with much disgust and trepidation. Suddenly he turns and shoves the food he's holding at MENCH, who jumps away. They laugh. Then MUG turns serious, saying to MENCH:*

**MUG:** See ee corpso, ditto mee moom-eye et pop-eye. [If I die, tell my mom and dad.]

**MENCH:** *(solemnly)* Bo bo. Tra la. Bee bee. [Goodbye. Good luck.]

*MUG takes the tiny amount in his fingers and places it in his mouth. A slight pause. He seems to enjoy it. But then he starts to react: he goes into convulsions, gasping and screaming. He is hamming it up for MENCH and she loves it. Finally, after many death rattles, groans, and spasms, he is "dead." MENCH takes his pulse and pronounces him "dead."*

Chay corpso. [He's dead.]

*Suddenly MUG is up again. The dead have risen; he is a horrible ghoul.*

**MUG:** Ee bee zombo! [I'm a zombie!]

*He is a walking corpse, sniffing the air angrily.*

Ee vancha da gourda da Nicknick . . . Ee vancha da gourda da Nicknick. [I want the bowl of Nick . . . I want the bowl of Nick.]

*Before NICK can react, MUG has grabbed the bowl and holds it over his head.*

Sisco la glowba. Corpsa la gourda da Nicknick! [Save the world. Kill the bowl of Nick!]

> *MUG bends the bowl on top of his head. It breaks in two. He is startled for an instant but quickly sees the humour in it and gets MENCH laughing too.*

**NICK:** You broke it!

**MUG:** Gros bos. [Big deal.]

> *MUG tosses the pieces to NICK.*

**MENCH:** Ee bee joost ein gourda, Nicknick. [It's just a bowl, Nick.]

**NICK:** You broke my bowl.

**MUG:** Aw, post a itsi Nicknick. [Oh, poor little Nick.]

**NICK:** You don't know what that was, you idiot!

> *NICK grabs MUG. MUG throws NICK on the floor.*

**MUG:** Sue es logo. Toota des Homelander say logo. Sue Sgak. [You're crazy. All the Homelanders are crazy. You Sgak.*]

**MENCH:** *(shocked)* Mog!

---

* "Sgak" represents a variety of cultural/racial slurs infamous in the English vocabulary.

MUG: Sgak!

*MUG exits.*

NICK: . . . He broke my bowl.

MENCH: Donax regretto. Mog joost tantra. [Don't worry about it. Mug just got mad.]

NICK: Why did he do that?

MENCH: Or bay sue-she? [Are you okay?]

NICK: That was my good bowl.

MENCH: Ee besta zet nama. Tra la. [I'd better go now. Bye.]

*MENCH exits.*

NICK: *(to audience)* I just went home. I didn't wait for school to get out. I just left.

*NICK's MOTHER enters and sits by the window. NICK looks in at her through the window, then decides to go in, hiding the broken bowl.*

MOTHER: Oh, you're home, Nick. Hi.

NICK: Hi.

MOTHER: How was your first day of school?

NICK: Okay.

MOTHER: Meet any nice kids?

NICK: Sure, lots.

MOTHER: You must be doing well in school, they let you out early.

NICK: Yeah, they let me out early.

MOTHER: What's that?

NICK: What?

MOTHER: That.

NICK: What?

MOTHER: That. In your hand.

NICK: Nothing.

MOTHER: Nick.

NICK: A bowl.

MOTHER: That's the bowl your friends in Homeland gave you.

NICK: Yeah.

MOTHER: How did it get broken?

NICK: Dropped it.

MOTHER: You dropped it. How?

NICK: I dunno. Playing.

MOTHER: What happened?

NICK: I fell in the playground.

MOTHER: How did you fall?

NICK: I slipped.

MOTHER: Slipped. On what?

NICK: On a . . . a . . . banana peel.

MOTHER: Are you telling me the truth?

NICK: Yes.

MOTHER: Come over here, young man, and look me in the eye.

NICK: Mom.

*NICK goes to her and she looks him in his eyes.*

MOTHER: Okay. Now say it.

NICK: I slipped on a banana peel.

**MOTHER:** Nick, why are you lying to me?

**NICK:** I'm not lying. You're the one who lied.

**MOTHER:** Nick, come on.

**NICK:** You told me I could learn to speak English in a week. It'll take forever! They talk so fast—blah, blah, blah—I don't even know what they're saying. I don't know what they want. Everything you said about this place was lies!

**MOTHER:** . . . Nick, what's the matter?

**NICK:** Do you know what sgak means?

**MOTHER:** Sgak. I don't know.

**NICK:** It's a bad word.

**MOTHER:** I don't know. Where did you hear it?

**NICK:** I was in a fight and this guy called me . . .

**MOTHER:** A fight? Did anyone get hurt?

**NICK:** No, this kid hates me. I hate him. I hate school. I hate Canada. I wanna go home.

**MOTHER:** I'm sure he doesn't hate you.

**NICK:** How do you know, were you there?

**MOTHER:** It's your first day at school. Remember, you're as strange to them as they are to you, right?

**NICK:** Yeah.

**MOTHER:** So if anyone bothers you, just ignore them. And Nick?

**NICK:** What?

**MOTHER:** I'll fix your bowl.

**NICK:** Okay.

**MOTHER:** Okay.

*MOTHER exits.*

**NICK:** *(to audience)* So the next day, I went back to school, but I wasn't very happy about it. I just did what Mom said and tried to ignore them.

*Enter MENCH with a bag of sports equipment. NICK turns away, ignoring her.*

**MENCH:** Lo, Nicknick. Sue vancha planch? [Hi, Nick. Do you want to play?]

*She notices that his back is turned from her and that he is looking up. She goes over to him and tries to see what he's looking at.*

Kel gander shtat? Kel matso? Nicknick? [What are you looking at? What's the matter? Nick?]

*She goes back to her sports bag, going through some of the things inside.*

Ee brognay gorbso sportso eekwippo. Gander. Ein, doos, tweet . . . [I brought gobs of sports equipment. Look. One, two, three . . . ]

*NICK continues to ignore her.*

*(in frustration)* Sue nax vancha planch, sue nax vancha planch. [Well, if you don't want to play, you don't want to play.]

*She gives up and sneaks behind NICK. NICK turns around and doesn't see her. Thinking MENCH has left, NICK goes to her sports bag. MENCH shadows him. He looks inside the bad, takes out a baseball. As he takes it out, he notices that MENCH is hiding behind him. He stands up and walks in intricate circles, making MENCH struggle not to be seen. He tosses the ball back and forth, making her run frantically as she tries to keep up with him and not be seen. Finally he throws the ball behind him and MENCH inadvertently catches it, revealing herself. NICK looks at her. They both laugh.*

Lo, Nicknick. [Hi, Nick.]

**NICK:** Lo, Menchamencha. [Hi, Menchmench.]

**MENCH:** Nax. [No.]

*Holding up one finger.*

Mencha.

**NICK:** Nax. [No.]

*Holding up one finger.*

Nick.

**MENCH:** Nick?

**NICK:** Nick.

*MENCH hits herself on the head.*

**MENCH:** Ohhh, yo.

**NICK:** Yo.

*MENCH hands NICK the glove.*

**MENCH:** Ee bee gerse glob glubber, Nick. [This is a baseball mitt, Nick.]

**NICK:** Gerse glob glubber.

**MENCH:** Bay perfecto! Nama . . . [That's perfect! Now . . . ]

*MENCH throws the ball. NICK catches it bare-handed.*

Nax. Sue usta gerse glob glubber por kitz da gerse glob. [No. You use the baseball mitt to catch the baseball.]

NICK: I understand . . .

*MENCH notices that NICK hasn't even put the mitt on.*

MENCH: Nax, dos finger eight donk inksta gerse glob glubber. Cor cheesy. [No, your fingers go inside the glove. Like this.]

NICK: Cor cheesy? [Like this?]

MENCH: Yo. [Yes.]

*MENCH throws the ball again. This time, NICK tries to use the mitt to hit the ball and sends it flying.*

Nax, nax, sue usta gerse glob glubber por kitz da gerse glob. Nax shlam shtat. [No, no, you use the baseball mitt for catching the ball. Not hitting it.]

*She demonstrates.*

NICK: I understand.

MENCH: Ay? [Eh?]

NICK: Oh. Yo, yo! [Yes, yes!]

MENCH: Sue-she. [Okay.]

*MENCH throws NICK a pop fly. NICK catches it.*

Kwee-sin-art! [Excellent!]

NICK: Yo! [Yeah!]

MENCH: Kitz! [Catch!]

NICK: Bliss-tex! [All right!]

*(to audience)* So I started to make friends. I learned how to catch popshees . . .

*He catches a fly ball.*

. . . and throw gutter globs . . .

*He throws MENCH a ground ball.*

. . . and how to put someone out at first . . .

*He catches the ball and tags out an imaginary runner.*

MENCH: Sewer rat! [You're out!]

NICK: And I learned how to play shlamshtick.

*MENCH hands NICK a hockey stick and they both pretend to skate, passing the invisible puck back and forth.*

MENCH: Nama! [Now!]

*She passes to NICK.*

NICK: Spinarama! [Turnaround!]

*NICK shoots.*

Chay chost! Chay shlamit! Chay scoro! [He shoots! He scores!] Yo!
Ee bee Grain Wetsky! [Yeah! It's Wayne Gretzky!]

*They slap hands triumphantly, then hold hands in pain.*

*(to audience)* And I learned to eat good Canadian foods, like—

*MENCH throws a basketball to NICK.*

MENCH: Baykee lassee!

*NICK catches the ball.*

NICK: Hot dogs!

*He throws it back.*

MENCH: Grosta mack!

*MENCH throws it to NICK.*

NICK: Hamburgers!

*NICK throws it back.*

**MENCH:** Greesee spudniks!

*MENCH throws to NICK.*

**NICK:** French fries!

*NICK throws it back.*

**MENCH:** Chubbee Blubber!

*MENCH throws to NICK.*

**NICK:** Double Bubble!

*NICK throws it back.*

**MENCH:** Tweet shtay mik freezee moomoo mik cheetah chumps, mik bakee sludge, mik wing wong, mik snikker giggle la tip top.

*She throws to NICK.*

**NICK:** Three scoops of ice cream with bananas, hot fudge, peanuts . . .

*He throws the ball to MENCH.*

. . . and a giant Snickers bar on top.

*MENCH throws the ball back and it hits him in the stomach. NICK groans.*

And stomach aches . . . and I got a Nickee jocko.

*MENCH helps him put on a nylon jacket that has an adapted Nike logo.*

I was doing pretty good. And my English? I could speak . . .

**MENCH:** Sue-she. [So-so.]

*MUG enters carrying a baseball bat. He ignores NICK.*

**MUG:** Lo, Mencha. [Hi, Mench.]

**MENCH:** Lo, Mog. [Hi, Mug.]

*MUG and MENCH play with the bat, gripping it hand over hand.*

**NICK:** Hi, Mug.

*MUG ignores NICK.*

**MUG:** Checka may gerse glob gipper. Sue vancha pranta boont, Mencha? [Check out my baseball bat. Want to practise bunting, Mench?]

**MENCH:** Sue-she, mo kitza. [Okay, I'll catch.]

**NICK:** Mo tossta! [I'll pitch!]

**MUG:** Nax. [No.]

**MENCH:** Ay? [What?]

**MUG:** Nax mit chay. [Not with him.]

**MENCH:** Kway nax? [Why not?]

**MUG:** May pop-eye dichay nax plancha mit chay. [My dad said not to play with him.]

**MENCH:** Sue pop-eye? [Your dad?]

**NICK:** Your dad won't let you play with me? Why not—kway nax?

**MUG:** Porska. [Because.]

**MENCH:** Kway nax? [Why not?]

**MUG:** Porska. [Because.]

**MENCH:** Kway nax, Mog? [Why not, Mug?]

**NICK:** Kway nax, Mog? [Why not, Mug?]

**MUG:** Porska sue es sgak. [Because you're a sgak.]

**MENCH:** Mog!

**NICK:** Because I'm a sgak. What does that mean? Kwel doe sgak mos? [What does sgak mean?]

*MUG pokes NICK with his bat.*

MUG: Sgak mos ee kat vos grute. [Sgak means I hate your guts.]

*MUG sniffs and coughs.*

Poo! Kway dis Homelanders fumato see fay? [Why do these Homelanders stink so much?]

MENCH: Sue nax comica, Mog. [You're not funny, Mug.]

*MUG tries to lighten things up.*

MUG: Vancha planch, Mencha? [Want to play, Mench?]

MENCH: Nax. [No.]

MUG: Ay? [What?]

MENCH: Nax! Nax mik sue. [No! Not with you.]

*MUG still tries to make MENCH respond, but she pulls away and stands beside NICK.*

MUG: Mencha . . . Mencha.

*(to NICK)* Sgak!

*MUG exits.*

MENCH: *(to NICK)* Tosta! [Throw the ball!]

NICK: Mench, what does sgak mean?

MENCH: Kwit? [What?]

NICK: Sorry. Kwel doe sgak mos? [What does sgak mean?]

MENCH: Sgak?

NICK: Yo! [Yes!]

*MENCH is very uncomfortable. Silence.*

Well, tell me. Deetmo. [Tell me.]

MENCH: Nax. [No.]

NICK: Kwel doe sgak mos? [What does Sgak mean?]

MENCH: Ee besta zet nama. [I'd better go now.]

NICK: Look, it's important. Kwel doe sgak mos? [What does Sgak mean?]

*Pause.*

MENCH: Homelander.

NICK: Homelander? Why do they call us that? Kway? [Why?]

MENCH: Porska chay kat Homelanders. Ee besta zet nama. [Because they hate Homelanders. I'd better go now.]

NICK: They hate Homelanders? Kway? [Why?]

*MENCH picks up her sports bag.*

MENCH: Tra la. [Bye.]

*She exits.*

NICK: It's not fair.

*NICK goes home.*

Dad! Dad!

*MOTHER enters.*

Where's Dad, Mom?

MOTHER: He's at work.

NICK: He's always at work. He's never at home anymore.

MOTHER: You should be happy he has work at all.

NICK: Yeah, but he's not working as a teacher.

MOTHER: No.

NICK: Why not? He is a teacher.

MOTHER: Not in Canada.

NICK: I never get to see him.

**MOTHER:** I know, neither do I.

**NICK:** Mom, what's the matter?

**MOTHER:** I just came back from the store and I'm not going back there. You'll have to do the shopping from now on.

**NICK:** Why? What happened?

**MOTHER:** I was leaving the store with my groceries when this man came up and started yelling at me.

**NICK:** Yelling at you? Why?

**MOTHER:** I didn't know why, and then other people started yelling and pointing.

**NICK:** What were they saying?

**MOTHER:** I didn't understand. I got so nervous I dropped the grocery bags, everything spilled on the floor—the eggs, the flour, the milk. They thought I was a fool.

**NICK:** You're not a fool, Mom.

**MOTHER:** Maybe they thought I was stupid. I don't know. I didn't understand. I just left all the food there. Oh, I miss Homeland so much. I wish I was there.

NICK: Mom, we haven't been here long. If someone's bothering you, just ignore them. Remember, you're as strange to them as they are to you, right?

*Pause.*

MOTHER: You're right, Nick. I'd better go.

*She starts to go.*

NICK: Where?

MOTHER: Back to get my groceries.

NICK: But you don't even know what to say.

MOTHER: You're right. You teach me.

NICK: Okay . . . Ee gobba may grokos, ee gibba may grund.

MOTHER: What does that mean?

NICK: I'm the idiot who spilled the groceries.

MOTHER: Nick!

NICK: Just kidding, Mom. It really means: "I've come for my groceries, give them to me please." Repeat after me: ee gobba may grokos.

MOTHER: *(botching it)* Eee gobble my gekos.

NICK: Grokos.

MOTHER: Grokos.

NICK: Good. Now: ee gibba may grund.

MOTHER: Giggle my ground.

NICK: No, gibba may grund. Ee gobba may grokos, ee gibba may grund.

MOTHER: Ee gobble my grekos, ee giggle my grunt.

NICK: Uh, Mom . . .

MOTHER: Give me my groceries, I've got a gun.

NICK: Mom!

MOTHER: Just kidding, Nick. Ee gobba may grokos, ee gibba may grund.

NICK: Good.

MOTHER: Thanks, Nick.

   *MOTHER exits.*

NICK: Good luck, Mom.

*MENCH looks in the window. She has the hockey mask on and plays monster, scratching on the glass. NICK hears her and goes to the window, calmly watching her. Realizing that she has not scared him, MENCH takes off the mask. Seeing her face, NICK screams and holds his heart. They laugh. MENCH holds a basketball.*

**MENCH:** Sue vancha droob da bolo mik mo? [Do you want to dribble the ball with me?]

**NICK:** Yo, ver shur. [Yes, for sure.]

**MENCH:** Kitz! [Catch!]

**NICK:** Gander dis, Mencha. [Look at this, Mench.]

*NICK shows off with the ball. MENCH takes her turn with the ball.*

**MENCH:** Gander dis. [Look at this.]

*NICK takes the ball, positions to shoot.*

**NICK:** Shotta tobasco? [Should I take a shot?]

**MENCH:** Yo! [Yes!]

**NICK:** Mo einst. [Me first.]

**MENCH:** Me doost. [Me second.]

*NICK gets set to shoot. MUG enters.*

MUG: Ay, homer, tosca da glob ta may. [Hey, homie, toss the ball to me.]

*MUG grabs the ball away from NICK.*

MENCH: Lear corpso. [Drop dead.]

MUG: Nax, ee vancha planch. [No, I want to play.]

*MUG goes to shoot at the basket, holding the ball over his head. NICK quickly snatches the ball away, holds it behind him so MENCH can take it. She hides it behind her back. MUG whirls around, looking for the ball. He looks at NICK.*

Tosca da glob. [Toss me the ball.]

*NICK shrugs and shows his empty hands. MUG shoves NICK aside and looks at MENCH, who smiles, revealing the ball and offering it to him. MUG smiles back, figuring he is in control again and that MENCH is back on his side. MUG goes to take the ball from MENCH.*

Gibba may. [Give it to me.]

MENCH: Nax, cue sue tornst. [No, wait your turn.]

*She tosses the ball over MUG's head to NICK.*

**MUG:** *(to MENCH)* Chay sue valentino, Mencha? [Is he your boy-friend, Mench?]

*MUG makes a smooching sound. Then he sniffs:*

Sue fumato como Homelander. [You smell like a Homelander.]

**MENCH:** Clampit! [Shut up!]

**MUG:** *(to NICK)* Gibba may da glob. [Give me the ball.]

**NICK:** Nax, Mog. [No, Mug.]

*NICK throws the ball through MUG's legs to MENCH.*

**MUG:** *(to MENCH)* Gibba may. [Give it to me.]

**MENCH:** Nax vay, row-zhay. [No way, Jose.]

*She fakes MUG out a few times with the ball, making him jump around and then fall to the ground, then effortlessly tosses it to NICK.*

**MUG:** *(to NICK)* Gibba may! [Give it to me!]

*MUG charges at NICK. NICK tries to get the ball away but MUG has his arm around his neck, choking him. MENCH runs over and drags MUG by the hair away from NICK. MUG grabs MENCH's arm and pulls it around into a half nelson. MENCH squirms in pain.*

*(to NICK)* Gibba may. [Give it to me.]

> *Slight pause. MUG twists harder.*

Gibba may. [Give it to me.]

> *NICK gives MUG the ball. He lets MENCH go.*

Taka. [Thank you.]

> *MUG starts to dribble the ball. Then he stops, turns to NICK:*

Sue vancha planch? [You want to play?]

> *MUG winds up as if to throw the ball at NICK full force, then stops, faking him out. Pause. MUG looks at MENCH. She turns away. MUG hands the ball to NICK. NICK goes to take it and MUG drops it on the ground and runs off. Slight pause.*

**NICK:** Es sue bay sue-she? [Are you okay?]

**MENCH:** Yo. [Yes.]

**NICK:** Maybe you shouldn't hang around me anymore.

**MENCH:** Kwit? [What?]

**NICK:** Me bay shnyden seesaw mik mo nama. [Maybe you shouldn't hang around me anymore.]

**MENCH:** Kway nax? [Why not?]

NICK: Homelanders are dangerous to your health . . . ee bee sgak!

MENCH: Gros bos. [Big deal.]

NICK: *(to audience)* I liked her. She was a real friend.

*(to MENCH)* Sue vanchen gander me hasa? [You want to see my house?]

MENCH: Nax jesto? [For sure?]

NICK: Kway nax? [Why not?]

MENCH: Kway nax? [Why not?]

*They go to NICK's house and enter.*

NICK: Mom!

*MOTHER enters.*

MOTHER: Who's this?

MENCH: Lo, ee be meegro Nick. [Hi, I'm Nick's friend.]

NICK: This is my best friend, Mom.

MOTHER: You didn't tell me you were bringing somebody home.

NICK: She's just my friend. Her name is Mench.

MOTHER: She's Canadian, isn't she?

NICK: Uh huh.

MENCH: Ee noma Mencha. Ee bee ha-ha doe matchay sue. [My name is Mench. I am pleased to meet you.]

MOTHER: Pardon me?

NICK: Chay noma Mencha. Chay bee ha-ha doe matchay sue. [Her name is Mench. She's pleased to meet you.]

MENCH: Ver shur. [For sure.]

MOTHER: I don't understand.

NICK: Chay noma Mencha, chay bee ha-ha doe matchay sue. [Her name is Mench, she's pleased to meet you.]

MOTHER: I don't understand, speak in Homelander to me.

NICK: But I can't with her here. She only speaks English.

MOTHER: Speak Homelander.

NICK: English.

MOTHER: Homelander!

NICK: English!

**MENCH:** Ee besta zet nama. [I'd better go now.]

*MENCH runs out.*

**NICK:** Nax, Mencha! [No, Mench!]

*(to MOTHER)* Good work, Mom. Thanks a lot.

**MOTHER:** I'm sorry, Nick. But I didn't say you could bring a Canadian into my house.

**NICK:** But we live in Canada. My friends are Canadian—yours are all Homelanders. Why are you so afraid of Mencha? Why wouldn't you speak English with her?

**MOTHER:** I'll speak English when I want to speak English, but I don't have to in my own home. Outside we can be like them but in here we keep our traditions.

**NICK:** Does that mean I can't bring my friends home?

**MOTHER:** You can have Homelander friends here.

**NICK:** Well, she isn't Homelander and she is my friend. She almost got her arm broken standing up for me.

**MOTHER:** What?

**NICK:** This bully started picking on me again and she stood up to him.

MOTHER: You mean that girl who was just here?

NICK: Yeah.

MOTHER: The Canadian girl stood up for you?

NICK: Yeah, and then he started twisting her arm.

MOTHER: Is she all right?

NICK: Yeah, she is now. Can't you see why I brought her home?

MOTHER: Yes. Of course . . . I'm sorry, Nick. Look—please—go and bring her in.

*NICK runs outside. MENCH has been waiting.*

NICK: Mencha. Mencha!

MENCH: Ee bee hee bee. [I'm still here.]

NICK: Co mosto! [Come on!]

MENCH: Ver shur? [Are you sure?]

NICK: Yo yo! [Yeah!]

*They go into the house.*

MOTHER: Nick, please tell her I'm sorry. Thank her and ask if her arm is all right.

**NICK:** *(to MENCH)* May moom-eye deetchay taka, et comes bilbo. [My mom says thanks, and wonders how your arm is.]

**MENCH:** Ee bee banzai. [It's fine.]

**MOTHER:** *(relieved)* Good.

**MENCH:** . . . Good.

   *MOTHER is delighted at her attempt to speak Homelander.*

**MOTHER:** Good!

   *MENCH is delighted at her success.*

**MENCH:** Good!

**NICK:** Good! . . . Her name is Mencha, Mom.

**MOTHER:** Mencha—please sit down . . . so you go to school with Nick, Mencha?

**MENCH:** Good!

**MOTHER:** . . . Ask Mencha if she likes school.

**NICK:** Abba sue lak skoss? [Do you like school?]

**MENCH:** Skoss? Ee kat skoss. Skoss fumato. Skoss abba may puko! [School? I hate school. School stinks. School makes me puke!]

NICK: . . . She says it's okay.

MOTHER: Ask her if she wants some of my special pudding.

NICK: Sue vancha globbalos Homelander? Ee bee gusto. [You want some Homelander pudding? It's good.]

MENCH: *(politely)* Nax, taka. [No, thank you.]

NICK: She says she'd love some.

MOTHER: Good. I'll be right back.

*MOTHER goes to get it. MENCH turns on NICK.*

MENCH: Nick! Taka moosaka! [Nick! Thanks a lot!]

NICK: Ee bee gusto gusto. [It's delicious.]

*MOTHER enters with the bowl.*

MOTHER: Here you go, Mencha.

MENCH: *(hesitantly)* Taka. [Thank you.]

*MENCH smiles at MOTHER, then turns to NICK and glares.*

MOTHER: Nick, tell her she doesn't have to eat it if she doesn't like it.

NICK: Nax gusto, nax muncho. [If you don't like it, don't eat it.]

*MENCH stares at him, then smiles at MOTHER. Pause. She smiles at MOTHER again. She looks at the bowl. Takes a little on her spoon. Tastes it. Pause. She does not react. She takes another spoonful. Tastes it. Pause. She instantly wolfs the rest of it down, scraping the bowl with her spoon, then lifting it to lick off the remainder. With her face still in the bowl, she looks up at MOTHER. Slight pause. MENCH puts down the bowl and whispers in NICK's ear. NICK whispers back.*

**MENCH:** *(haltingly)* Kick me, please.

*NICK kicks her.*

**MOTHER:** What?

**MENCH:** *(more forcefully)* Kick me, please.

*NICK shrugs, kicks her again.*

**MOTHER:** Nick!

*NICK whispers in MENCH's ear. MENCH hands MOTHER the bowl.*

**MENCH:** More, please.

**MOTHER:** *(delighted)* Come with me.

*MOTHER and MENCH exit together.*

**NICK:** *(to audience)* I felt great. Mom liked Mencha and Mencha liked Mom. They got along like, like they were from the same country. But not Mog. He still didn't like me. Whenever he had a chance he'd call me names. And now that I spoke a little English, I knew what he meant and I hated it. And then one day:

*MUG sneaks to the window and begins writing on it with lip-stick. MOTHER enters, sees him.*

**MOTHER:** Nick!

*NICK enters, sees him.*

**NICK:** Mog!

*MUG runs off.*

**MOTHER:** Do you know that boy?

**NICK:** Yeah.

**MOTHER:** Who is he? Why did he write this?

**NICK:** He's the one I told you about.

**MOTHER:** Is this the word, sgak?

**NICK:** That's what they call us.

**MOTHER:** Well, you'd better give me his name.

**NICK:** No.

MOTHER: Why not?

NICK: I want to work this out myself.

MOTHER: But you could get hurt.

NICK: I know, but he's not the first bully I've ever met. They're every-where, even in Homeland. Picking on people is an international sport.

MOTHER: So what are you going to do?

NICK: Well, if it's an international sport, I guess I'll just have to play it.

MOTHER: Nick, don't get into trouble.

NICK: . . . Okay, Mom.

*MOTHER exits.*

*(to audience)* I tried all kinds of things to get Mog to leave me alone.

*MUG enters.*

MUG: Lo, sgak. [Hello, sgak.]

NICK: I wouldn't let it bother me. In fact, I just pretended I liked it.

*(to MUG)* Taka, taka. [Thank you, thank you.]

*MUG turns away, puzzled.*

I just pretended he was calling me handsome and intelligent.

MUG: Sgak. Sgak!

*NICK smiles at MUG.*

NICK: Taka moosaka. Taka scaree moosh. [Thanks very much. Many big thanks.]

*MUG is frustrated and tries again.*

MUG: Sgaaaaaaaaaaaaak!!

*NICK points inside MUG's mouth.*

NICK: Nax brusho da tooto! [You didn't brush your teeth!]

*MUG turns away, holding his mouth. MENCH enters.*

MENCH: Nick!

NICK: *(to audience)* Mencha helped.

Lo. [Hi.]

MENCH: Lo. [Hi.]

*NICK asks if she wants to help with MUG.*

NICK: Yo? [Yes?]

*MENCH agrees to help.*

MENCH: Yo. [Yes.]

NICK: *(to audience)* Sometimes we ignored him.

MUG: Sgak sgakky sgakky sgak, Nick scrunt un Sgak spit. [Nick is a sgakky sgak . . . ]

*NICK and MENCH ignore MUG. MUG turns away.*

NICK: And once . . .

MUG: Sgaaak!

NICK: . . . we just stared right through him.

*NICK and MENCH both go bug-eyed at MUG, startling him. MUG turns away.*

Once he just happened to bump me.

*MUG walks in a small circle whistling, and bumps NICK.*

So I just happened to bump him back.

*NICK also walks in a circle, whistling, then he bumps MUG. MUG goes flying.*

And another time . . .

*MUG is swinging his baseball bat.*

. . . we just ran.

*MUG chases MENCH and NICK. At the end of the chase, NICK stops to face MUG.*

And another time, I just stayed there.

*NICK stands his ground. MUG waves the bat, threatening to smash NICK, but NICK won't budge, looking MUG in the eye. Finally MUG backs down. He lowers the bat and casually plays with it, as if he had other plans for it altogether, though he knows he has lost.*

At home, my parents are taking English lessons. They learned it in a week—well, sort of. I still speak Homelander. I don't want to forget it. So now I have two languages, English and Homelander. And Mug? We're even going to play on the same shlamshtick team.

*MENCH hands NICK and MUG hockey sticks.*

And you know, I think everything's going to be okay . . .

*MUG and NICK get ready to face off. MENCH blows the whistle. MUG raises the stick high, ready to smash NICK.*

. . . maybe.

# INVISIBLE KIDS

*Invisible Kids* was first produced by Unicorn Theatre for Children in January 1985 at the Arts Theatre in London, England, with the following company:

Georgie: Tracy Harper
Vince: George Lascelles
Chris: Anthony Renshaw
Samantha: Josephine Welcome
Thiun: David Forman

Directed by Dennis Foon
Designed by Bernard Culshaw
Lighting by Angus Stewart

## STAGING NOTES

The playground: Based on the many examples seen throughout the city, the set should be a haphazard collection of platforms, ramps, ladders, ropes, and swings. The playground should provide the actors with unlimited possibilities for movement—and yet it should be instantly recognizable to the audience as something they themselves play on every day.

## THE MUSIC

Pop music that currently stands at the top of the charts is played at the beginning and end of the show and between the scenes. In this text I indicate the choices that were made for the original production. They are only meant to give an insight into the kind of mood and rhythm I hoped to achieve and should therefore be used only as a guideline—although Bob Marley's "One Love" is a classic that many kids seem to know and adore, so it may continue to be relevant to subsequent productions.

## PLAYERS

Georgie
Vince
Chris
Samantha
Ranem

They are all about eleven or twelve years old.
Chris is the only child who is meant to be visibly "white."

## SETTING

A playground in Toronto, present time.

## TOPICALITY

It is of extreme importance that every aspect of the production reflect today's reality. Choices of clothing and music should be made based on current kids' culture—a quickly evolving phenomenon. Many of the choices of language and references in this play will also need constant updating by production theatres to ensure that the production is in step with the local region and current trends.

# SCENE ONE

*As the lights come up and the music fades out, we hear a
booming Tarzan ape call. Suddenly, GEORGIE enters, swinging
across the jungle gym.*

**GEORGIE:** Jane, Jane, don't worry, I'll save you, don't worry, girl!
AHK! Crocodiles! Take that, you ugly lizard, you! Stab, stab, stab! I
know you're dead 'cause you're floating with your belly up—belly
up means you're dead meat.

*She is attacked by another one.*

AH! Jane, Jane, Jane and Boy, calling Jane and Boy, Jane and Boy
come in, Jane and Boy, I'm dying, the crocks got me, Tarzan is
dying, the great Tarzan of the jungle is sinking fast, he's ah, ah,
ah . . .

*While GEORGIE has been playing Tarzan, assuming she was
unobserved, VINCE has entered and has been watching her
all the while. He now interrupts her death scene, making the
sound of an ambulance siren.*

**VINCE:** Whee-uh, whee-uh, whee-uh! Get him on the stretcher,
boys, gotta save Tarzan before he bleeds to death.

GEORGIE: I'm doing just fine, thank you.

VINCE: We saw the accident, sir. Run over by a green crocodile. Vicious things.

GEORGIE: I'm not dying, all right?

VINCE: He needs a transfusion, prepare the needle. Tarzan, old pal, would you mind holding still while we give you a few gallons of blood?

GEORGIE: I don't want any blood.

VINCE: He's delirious. The fever.

GEORGIE: Vince!

VINCE: *(as official)* Give him a large injection to settle him down.

*(as underling)* How strong, sir?

*(as official)* Gorilla strength.

> VINCE *holds* GEORGIE *down, preparing her for the injection.*

GEORGIE: Vince!

VINCE: . . . What?

GEORGIE: Chill out. That's enough.

VINCE: Oh. Sorry, Georgie.

GEORGIE: That's all right, Vince.

VINCE: Thank you, Georgie.

GEORGIE: You're welcome, Vince.

VINCE: Thank you for saying "you're welcome," Georgie.

GEORGIE: That's enough, Vince.

VINCE: All right, Georgie.

GEORGIE: All right! . . . Where's everybody?

VINCE: I don't know. But they'll show up.

GEORGIE: Yes, but when?

VINCE: When they're ready.

GEORGIE: But that means we have to wait.

VINCE: Yes.

GEORGIE: I hate waiting. My mother always says, "Be patient, be patient." I feel like I have to be patient so much I'm turning into a patient. They might as well put me into the hospital.

**VINCE:** I just tried to put you into the hospital: you wouldn't go . . . We could count while we wait.

**GEORGIE:** I hate it! I have to wait for everything. Wait for your friends, wait till you grow up. All we do is wait, wait, wait.

**VINCE:** What do you want to count to?

**GEORGIE:** First one to count to three thousand is the winner.

**VINCE:** I have to count to three thousand?

**GEORGIE:** Or more if it takes that long.

**VINCE:** Really?

**GEORGIE:** Yes, three thousand. And maybe more.

**VINCE:** What comes after 999,999?

**GEORGIE:** What?

**VINCE:** I just want to be sure I know what happens if they take a long, long time to show up.

**GEORGIE:** One million.

**VINCE:** One million and one, one million and two . . .

**GEORGIE:** Wait, you're supposed to start at one . . .

VINCE: Yeah but this way I get a head start. Million and three, million and four . . .

GEORGIE: You're cheating!

VINCE: I know, and you know, but they won't know.

GEORGIE: But starting at a million won't make them arrive any faster!

VINCE: Maybe, maybe not.

*CHRIS enters, eating a sweet.*

Hello, Christopher.

CHRIS: Hi, Vince.

VINCE: Want to count to two million?

GEORGIE: Hi, Christopher!

CHRIS: Hi . . .

*(to GEORGIE)* What are you doing on my jungle gym?

GEORGIE: It's not yours.

CHRIS: Yes, it is.

GEORGIE: It's everybody's.

CHRIS: Get off my spot, you big . . .

*CHRIS whispers something in her ear.*

GEORGIE: What?

CHRIS: You're sitting on my spot . . .

GEORGIE: What did you say?

CHRIS: . . . Nothing

GEORGIE: I heard what you said!

*CHRIS tries to get away, but GEORGIE leaps on his back and starts twisting his head.*

CHRIS: Ow, ow, let go of me!

GEORGIE: Not after what you said!

CHRIS: It was a joke!

GEORGIE: That word is no joke!

CHRIS: Vince, Vince, save me, Vince. She's killing me!

VINCE: All right then.

*VINCE doesn't move.*

Why are you killing him?

GEORGIE: 'Cause he hurt me.

CHRIS: I didn't hurt you.

GEORGIE: Yes, you did.

CHRIS: Ow! Now you're hurting me!

VINCE: He hurts you, now you're hurting him. Does it still hurt?

CHRIS: YES!

GEORGIE: Yes, it still hurts.

CHRIS: It does?

GEORGIE: Yes, it does.

CHRIS: Oh.

VINCE: What did he do?

GEORGIE: He called me a name.

CHRIS: So? Everybody calls everybody names.

VINCE: That's true.

GEORGIE: But what if you're a certain colour and they call you . . .

*GEORGIE whispers into VINCE's ear.*

**VINCE:** Get him!

*CHRIS runs under a platform. VINCE goes in for the kill.*

**CHRIS:** Hey, come on, hey, it wasn't that bad. People say it all the time. You just don't have a sense of humour . . . ow, ow . . .

**VINCE:** I haven't even hit you yet.

**CHRIS:** I know, I'm preparing myself. ow!

*SAMANTHA enters.*

**SAMANTHA:** Hey. Leave him alone.

**GEORGIE:** No way.

**SAMANTHA:** Fighting's not allowed on the playground.

**GEORGIE:** Yes, but you don't know what he said.

**SAMANTHA:** Doesn't matter. Fighting is against the rules.

**VINCE:** But he called her a name . . . he called her . . .

*VINCE whispers it to SAMANTHA.*

**SAMANTHA:** . . . Thank you. I'm going now to tell Mr. Thomas.

CHRIS: Hey, wait, stop. Don't tell, please, don't tell. I was just kidding. I didn't really mean it.

GEORGIE: But you said it.

CHRIS: It sort of slipped out of my mouth, that's all, like if chewing gum fell out.

GEORGIE: Not the same thing.

CHRIS: I know, I know, it was stupid, all right? It was a mistake. I'll never do it again.

VINCE: Really?

CHRIS: Really.

SAMANTHA: Really really?

CHRIS: Really really.

GEORGIE: I don't believe you!

CHRIS: I said I was sorry.

VINCE: He did say that.

GEORGIE: . . . All right.

SAMANTHA: Well, if that's all right with Georgie, it's all right with me . . . besides—I have some secret information.

**GEORGIE:** Secret?

**CHRIS:** What kind of secret?

**SAMANTHA:** I have secret information from Mr. Thomas.

**GEORGIE:** What?

**CHRIS:** What?

**VINCE:** What?

**SAMANTHA:** It's all on this piece of paper.

**GEORGIE:** Read it!

*Just before she can, RANEM enters.*

**CHRIS:** Hey, hold on. A spy.

**GEORGIE:** Who's he?

**VINCE:** I've never seen him before.

**SAMANTHA:** He's the new kid from Syria.

*VINCE and CHRIS go over to RANEM.*

**CHRIS:** What's your name?

**RANEM:** Ranem.

**VINCE:** Are you really from Syria?

**RANEM:** Yes. Damascus.

**CHRIS:** When did you leave?

**RANEM:** It is three years.

**VINCE:** What's Damascus like?

**RANEM:** Very old.

**CHRIS:** How old?

**RANEM:** Maybe four thousand years.

**CHRIS:** Nothing's that old.

**SAMANTHA:** No, it's true, I read about it.

**VINCE:** You speak English pretty well.

**CHRIS:** Not that well.

**VINCE:** That's 'cause he speaks Arabic too, right?

**RANEM:** Right. And some German. And Greek.

**CHRIS:** Really?

**RANEM:** Yes.

CHRIS: You do not.

GEORGIE: That makes four languages.

CHRIS: Prove it.

RANEM: How?

SAMANTHA: Say something in each language.

RANEM: What?

GEORGIE: Say, "Chris is a big fat zitbag."

CHRIS: What!

GEORGIE: Say, "Chris is a big ugly zitbag" in Arabic, German, and Greek.

CHRIS: No, no. Say, "Chris is a really handsome and smart guy."

*RANEM now speaks in each language, using the expression "CHRIS is a human being," or "CHRIS is a good boy."*

*RANEM speaks in Arabic.*

GEORGIE: That's Arabic, right?

*RANEM speaks in Greek.*

What was that?

RANEM: Greek . . .

*RANEM speaks in French.*

CHRIS: And that's German.

GEORGIE: Didn't sound like German.

RANEM: It was French. I learned a little French too . . .

*RANEM speaks in German.*

GEORGIE: Now that's German!

CHRIS: Where did you learn all that?

RANEM: It took a long time to come here. We had to travel, lived in different camps.

CHRIS: I went to summer camp. The mosquitoes are terrible.

SAMANTHA: Not that kind of summer camp, silly.

RANEM: Refugee camps.

VINCE: That must've been hard.

RANEM: Not easy.

GEORGIE: Well I think he's a genius.

CHRIS: No he's not. He doesn't speak English well.

RANEM: You speak Arabic?

CHRIS: No.

GEORGIE: Or German or French or Greek?

CHRIS: No.

GEORGIE: Well, when you do, let us know and you can be a genius too. And now that we know he's not a spy, tell us the secret, Samantha.

SAMANTHA: Are you ready?

ALL: Yes!

SAMANTHA: All right, then: I was helping in the office so Mr. Thomas let me have a copy early. This announcement won't be made until tomorrow.

GEORGIE: Read it!

*SAMANTHA clears her throat.*

SAMANTHA: Notice: One of our Grade Six students . . .

CHRIS: Who? Is that us?

GEORGIE: Who else—read it!

**SAMANTHA:** After much discussion over the uncertainty with border crossing, we have finally decided to allow the Grade Six class trip to take place . . .

**ALL:** YAY!

**SAMANTHA:** . . . Due to the fact that one of our students has been picked to present at the International Science Fair at Krystal Park.

**ALL:** Wow! Allll right!!

**GEORGIE:** Who was picked?

**SAMANTHA:** Ranem Al Shiakh.

**CHRIS:** Who's that?

*RANEM modestly raises his hand.*

You? But you just got to the school.

**SAMANTHA:** The cost of the trip will be twenty dollars.

**CHRIS:** Twenty bucks!

**SAMANTHA:** This includes return bus transportation and admission to the science fair.

**VINCE:** Krystal Park!

SAMANTHA: Your child is to take a bag lunch and sufficient pocket money for admission to the amusement park rides.

CHRIS: I'm going on Devil Mountain for five rides!

SAMANTHA: I'm going for ten! Devil Mountain!

RANEM: Devil Mountain?

CHRIS: It's a roller coaster—I hear it goes around in so many loops, people get sick on it. They even fall off and crash and get squashed and die on it.

SAMANTHA: And it's going to happen on my birthday! The greatest birthday present ever! I can't wait to go on Devil Mountain—I'm going to wear all my neon clothes when I go so you can see me like a light bulb when I'm zooming on the mountain. I'm going to wear my neon yellow top, my neon yellow pants, my neon green socks, and my neon pink shoes.

CHRIS: Don't forget your neon pink underpants!

SAMANTHA: Shut up!

CHRIS: Take your own advice.

GEORGIE: I just want to go to the science fair and see all the great projects.

CHRIS: I just hope my mom can spare the twenty bucks. That's a lot of moolah.

**RANEM:** Moolah?

**SAMANTHA:** *(to RANEM)* He means money.

**RANEM:** Moolah.

**GEORGIE:** Congratulations, Ranem!

**RANEM:** Thank you.

**GEORGIE:** No, thank you! It's all 'cause of you we get to go!

**SAMANTHA:** I'm going home to ask right now.

**CHRIS:** Me too!

**GEORGIE:** Me three!

> *SAMANTHA, GEORGIE, and CHRIS exit, leaving VINCE and RANEM on stage. VINCE hangs upside down.*

**VINCE:** . . . Hi.

**RANEM:** Hi.

**VINCE:** You like it around here?

**RANEM:** Yes, I think so.

**VINCE:** I don't. It's boring around here. Nothing to do. That's why I need a bike.

RANEM: A bike?

VINCE: I really have to get one. A BMX.

RANEM: BMX.

VINCE: Not just your regular BMX. This one's a Hutch. It has an alloy stem and full chrome plating and chromoly frame and forks.

RANEM: Alloy stem . . . full chro play . . .

VINCE: . . . and chromoly frame and forks. I really have to get one. I'm lonely without a bike. You have a bike?

RANEM: I had in Syria.

VINCE: You had a bike and you left it there?

RANEM: No room on the boat. Very crowded. One hundred people on boat as big as this.

VINCE: You'd have to sleep standing up!

RANEM: Right. Sometimes.

VINCE: How long were you on that boat?

RANEM: One, maybe two weeks. Till it sank.

VINCE: It sank?

**RANEM:** Yes. Ten people drowned. And my father and sister.

**VINCE:** That's horrible.

**RANEM:** Not easy. You go on class trip?

**VINCE:** Yeah. What did you invent for the science fair?

**RANEM:** A kite.

**VINCE:** What kind of kite?

**RANEM:** One that needs no wind.

**VINCE:** A kite can't fly with no wind.

**RANEM:** I can show you sometime.

**VINCE:** Okay! See you then.

*VINCE exits.*

**RANEM:** See you.

*RANEM exits. Blackout. Music.*

## SCENE TWO

*The lights come up into a half-light. As the music plays, we see*
*RANEM, SAMANTHA, and CHRIS enter; take out their lunches; and*
*start eating. As the lights fade up, the music fades out. SAMANTHA*
*immaculately sets out a napkin like a little tablecloth and precisely*
*sets out her lunch on it, drawing CHRIS's attention.*

SAMANTHA: What are you looking at?

CHRIS: Nothing.

SAMANTHA: Just because you're a slob doesn't mean I have to be one.

CHRIS: Hey, thingy, watch this. Bet they don't do this in Syria.

*CHRIS does some kind of gymnastic feat, perhaps some donkey*
*kicks. RANEM watches, and when CHRIS looks to him, RANEM*
*proceeds to top him, perhaps with a perfectly executed backflip.*

Not bad. But can you do this?

*Again CHRIS performs a gymnastic move and is totally out-*
*classed by RANEM, who brilliantly executes a series of flips.*

*(Important note: RANEM is never showing off, CHRIS is. RANEM never smirks at his success or seems proud of this small victory. He doesn't have to: the others do it for him.)*

But can you do this?

*CHRIS stands on his head. The others groan. RANEM stands on his head.*

**GEORGIE:** Oh, come on, Chris, anybody can do that.

*GEORGIE now stands on her head as well.*

**SAMANTHA:** I can do it. I can do it too.

*SAMANTHA tries to stand on her head but is having trouble.*

**GEORGIE:** Come on, Samantha, you can do it.

*SAMANTHA finally does it too. Now all four are standing on their heads.*

**SAMANTHA:** I did it, I did it!

*VINCE enters. He looks at the group of headstanders without reacting. Then he walks away.*

**GEORGIE:** Hi, Vince.

**CHRIS:** Hi, Vince.

RANEM: Hi, Vince.

SAMANTHA: Hello, Vincent.

VINCE: . . . Hi.

GEORGIE: We're all standing on our heads.

VINCE: Oh.

CHRIS: You stand on your head too.

VINCE: Not now, thanks.

GEORGIE: Oh, c'mon, Vince.

SAMANTHA: He doesn't know how. Vincent doesn't know how to stand on his head.

CHRIS: He knows how to stand on his head. He always stands on his head.

GEORGIE: What's wrong with you, Vincie?

VINCE: Nothing.

*GEORGIE starts to come down.*

GEORGIE: Something's wrong.

*The rest begin to come down too.*

CHRIS: Something wrong, Vince?

SAMANTHA: Maybe his mom and dad won't let him go on the class trip.

GEORGIE: Is that it, Vincie? Can't you go to Niagara Falls?

VINCE: Yeah, I can go.

RANEM: Something is wrong.

*VINCE nods.*

GEORGIE: Tell us.

VINCE: Yesterday, after school . . . walking home. There was this man walking his dog. A German shepherd. He called me a name.

CHRIS: What did he call you?

VINCE: The same thing you called her yesterday.

CHRIS: I said I was sorry. I'll never do it again.

VINCE: I know you won't. But he will.

CHRIS: But you're just a kid.

VINCE: He yelled, "Go back to your own country."

GEORGIE: He what?

SAMANTHA: But this is your country. You were born here.

CHRIS: Did you tell him? Did you tell him you were born in Canada?

VINCE: I wanted to, but I just kept walking. And then he yelled it again, "Go back to where you came from!" . . . But this is where I come from, this is my home, this is where I have always lived! . . . He knew that. He didn't care. He didn't like who I was . . . Then he took the leash off his big German shepherd and sent it after me.

CHRIS: What!

VINCE: It ran straight for me. Snapping, barking, teeth so big, trying to bite me. So I ran. And it was right behind me . . . No! I jumped on top of a car. It just waited. Seemed like hours and it was getting late. My parents would wonder where I was . . . then it looked like it was sleeping. Just lying there. So I started to climb off the car, quietly, quietly. Crossed the street—if I could just turn the corner, my house was just two streets away . . .

GEORGIE: Then what?

VINCE: When I got home and told my dad he was furious. He ran out looking for that man but he couldn't find him . . . I was afraid to go outside.

CHRIS: I could find that man. I'd find him and kill his dog.

GEORGIE: It's not the dog's fault.

SAMANTHA: It's the man who trained it. It's the man who sent it after Vincent.

VINCE: It's the man.

CHRIS: Then I'll find the man. And I'll kill him.

GEORGIE: Great, how are you going to do that?

CHRIS: Make a trap. I could do it.

GEORGIE: But what about all his friends? They're just like him. And hurting him would just give his friends an excuse to go after the rest of us.

VINCE: If I had a BMX I could have ridden away from that dog.

GEORGIE: Yeah, if you had a BMX.

SAMANTHA: But you don't have one.

VINCE: But if I had one I could have gotten away.

RANEM: No. Dog is faster. If you run, the dog will chase you.

CHRIS: What?

RANEM: Never run from dog.

CHRIS: You mean if a gigantic snarling beast is attacking you, you shouldn't try to get away?

**RANEM:** No. Never run.

**SAMANTHA:** You are cracked. If a monster drooling dog came after me, I'd run so fast you wouldn't see me.

**GEORGIE:** Me too.

**RANEM:** The dog would. Dog is faster than you. I can show you.

**VINCE:** What are you going to do?

**RANEM:** You be Vince. I can be dog.

**VINCE:** What?

**RANEM:** Ready?

**VINCE:** For what?

> *RANEM pretends to be a vicious dog and goes for VINCE. He is quite scary.*

Hey, come on now.

> *RANEM breaks out of his dog character for an instant in order to coach VINCE.*

**RANEM:** Don't be afraid. Don't move.

**VINCE:** What are you doing?

*RANEM becomes the dog again, totally ferocious. VINCE is terrified, tries to run away, but RANEM has him cornered.*

RANEM: All right. Try again. This time, be still.

VINCE: He's completely crazy.

RANEM: Ready?

*VINCE hesitates.*

GEORGIE: Go on, Vince.

CHRIS: Yeah.

VINCE: . . . All right then . . .

*RANEM comes after VINCE again. He barks like crazy but VINCE does not move. The dog starts to calm down.*

RANEM: You see, you give dog nothing, he has nothing to chase, nothing to bark at, nothing to fear . . . You can start to move.

*VINCE starts to walk away. RANEM barks madly.*

Never turn back on dog.

VINCE: Anything you say, boss.

RANEM: Walk backwards. Slowly.

*VINCE moves. RANEM snarls.*

Too fast.

**VINCE:** Sorry, sir.

**RANEM:** Pretty soon dog let you go.

*Finally VINCE escapes.*

**CHRIS:** Is that for real?

**GEORGIE:** Would that really work?

**RANEM:** Most of the time. Some dogs, no, but most dogs stop if you stop. Give them something, they get excited. If nothing to chase, nothing to fight, they stop.

**GEORGIE:** It's my turn. I get to do it too.

**SAMANTHA:** I get to do it too.

*SAMANTHA starts barking. The others also turn into dogs and all begin howling.*

**VINCE:** Did you bring your kite?

**RANEM:** Yes. Do you want to see?

**GEORGIE:** What kind of kite?

**VINCE:** His science fair project. It flies with no wind.

**CHRIS:** That's impossible.

**RANEM:** It is the shape. You pull, the air lifts it.

**CHRIS:** I know how to fly kites. You need a huge, monster wind.

**RANEM:** Not this kite.

> *RANEM pulls out a small kite, unreels a relatively short string, and begins expertly swooping the kite around. The kids stare amazed.*

**GEORGIE:** That's incredible!

**VINCE:** How'd you figure that out?

**RANEM:** No school in the camp. My mother taught me aerodynamics. She is an engineer.

**CHRIS:** Aero what?

**RANEM:** Aerodynamics. How solid things fly through air.

**CHRIS:** Oh, yeah, and what company does your mom work for?

**RANEM:** They won't let her be an engineer here, so she drives a taxi.

**GEORGIE:** What a waste!

**VINCE:** Can I try your kite?

**RANEM:** Yes . . . hold it like this. And move.

*VINCE, wide-eyed, flits the kite around. Then he runs off with it.*

**GEORGIE:** My turn!

**CHRIS:** Me!

**SAMANTHA:** Wait up!

*They all follow. Blackout. Music.*

## SCENE THREE

*From the blackout the lights fade up into a half-light. We see CHRIS enter, who is trying to jump through one leg. SAMANTHA has also entered. She sits and reads a book. GEORGIE enters and sits apart from the others, obviously upset. RANEM enters and watches CHRIS. The lights fade up full and the music fades out.*

**CHRIS:** I'm trying to hop through my leg. See, you gotta get this leg through here without letting go, like this. It's really difficult.

*Holding onto his right foot, CHRIS tries to hop over his right leg with his left foot. He is once again unsuccessful. RANEM holds his right foot, imitating CHRIS.*

Yeah, that's right . . .

*RANEM effortlessly hops over his leg.*

Yeah . . . like that. But—but—can you do this . . .

*CHRIS does a cartwheel.*

. . . with no hands.

*Slight pause.* RANEM *flips in the air, performing a cartwheel without using his hands.*

Well, yeah, that's . . . pretty good.

*VINCE enters. He is beaming with a huge grin.*

What are you smiling at? You think this is funny?

**RANEM:** Why are you smiling?

**VINCE:** She said "maybe."

**CHRIS:** Who said "maybe"?

**VINCE:** My mom. My mom said "maybe"!

**SAMANTHA:** That's very nice, Vincent. I'm very happy for you that your mother said maybe. Maybe what?

**VINCE:** Maybe she and Dad will get me that BMX.

**CHRIS:** No way. The one you want costs two hundred bucks.

**RANEM:** Lots of moolah.

**VINCE:** I asked them four hundred times. I asked my dad two hundred times and my mom two hundred and one times.

**SAMANTHA:** That makes four hundred and one.

VINCE: One for good luck.

CHRIS: How long have you been asking them?

VINCE: Forever. I've been asking them for a BMX forever.

SAMANTHA: And in total you have asked them four hundred and one times.

VINCE: Yesterday.

SAMANTHA: What?

VINCE: I asked them four hundred and one times yesterday. And I told them that I was going to ask them four hundred times a day until they got me a BMX. That's when Mom said "maybe."

SAMANTHA: I can see why.

CHRIS: They'll never buy you one.

VINCE: Maybe.

CHRIS: They just said "maybe" to shut you up.

VINCE: Maybe.

CHRIS: They don't have the money. They'll never buy you a BMX in a million years.

VINCE: Maybe.

CHRIS: They won't send you on the class trip and buy you a BMX.

VINCE: Maybe.

CHRIS: Stop saying "maybe"!

VINCE: Maybe.

CHRIS: Aaaargh!

SAMANTHA: I'm going on the class trip. I wouldn't miss it for the world. I'm going to ride the roller coaster five times. No, ten times. Did you bring your permission slips? Today is the deadline.

CHRIS: Yeah, I did.

VINCE: Me too.

*RANEM is silent.*

SAMANTHA: What about you, Georgie?

*GEORGIE scowls.*

Wouldn't your parents give you the money?

GEORGIE: Yeah, they would.

SAMANTHA: So are you going or not?

GEORGIE: I don't care.

CHRIS: What do you mean you don't care?

GEORGIE: I don't care if I go or not. I don't care about nothing.

SAMANTHA: That doesn't make sense. Nothing's nothing, so you can't care about nothing because nothing is nothing.

CHRIS: What are you talking about?

SAMANTHA: Nothing.

GEORGIE: Well, it is about something.

SAMANTHA: See, I told you!

GEORGIE: I just talked to Mr. Thomas. Ranem can't go to Krystal Park. Or the science fair.

VINCE: What? You didn't say a thing.

SAMANTHA: Is it true?

CHRIS: Your mom won't let you go?

RANEM: No, she wants me to go. But I can't cross the border.

GEORGIE: But you were invited. You made the magic kite.

RANEM: If you are Syrian, you need more magic than that.

GEORGIE: It's not fair.

SAMANTHA: It's just the way it is.

VINCE: That doesn't make it right.

CHRIS: Do they think you're a terrorist?

RANEM: We left Syria because of those people.

CHRIS: I can't stand this!

GEORGIE: It's not fair.

CHRIS: I want to do something. I'm going to beat somebody up. Tell me who is making this happen, Ranem. I'm going to find that jerk and smash his face in.

SAMANTHA: Yeah, you and whose army? It's not just one person, it's the government.

CHRIS: So what are we going to do?

VINCE: . . . Let's make a petition.

RANEM: A petition? For people to sign?

VINCE: Yes.

CHRIS: What'll we say on it?

VINCE: We'll say we do not think it is fair to keep Ranem the genius from going to the science fair.

**SAMANTHA:** And Krystal Park!

**GEORGIE:** Not just Ranem, everybody.

**VINCE:** We should all be treated the same.

**CHRIS:** Good.

**RANEM:** Yes.

**CHRIS:** All right, Georgie?

**GEORGIE:** All right. Who are you going to send it to?

**VINCE:** After we get, say, a thousand kids to sign, we'll send it to, to . . .

**CHRIS:** Drake.

**SAMANTHA:** You're really sad, you know that, Christopher? You have to send it to somebody who can do something. You have to send it to the prime minister and the president.

**GEORGIE:** The president?

**CHRIS:** He'd never listen to us.

**VINCE:** Maybe.

**SAMANTHA:** He might do something.

GEORGIE: Maybe . . . something.

*GEORGIE plays the president:*

Good morning, Christopher, great to meet you. Sorry, I don't shake hands, the germs. I'm a germaphobe and you should be one too. Oh! A petition, I love petitions! Give it here, I know just what to do with it.

*She grabs the imaginary papers from CHRIS and eats them.*

Umm, delicious, I love Big Macs!

CHRIS: You're eating our petition, sir.

GEORGIE: That's fake news—anyone can see it's a hamburger. Now go wash your hands.

CHRIS: Our friend is Syrian and he's a good person!

GEORGIE: It just takes one bad burger.

CHRIS: He's just a kid!

GEORGIE: And I bet he's a high-quality person. You can keep him. Keep 'em all! I love you kids! You're great! And I'm the greatest!

*The president waves goodbye with a big TV smile.*

CHRIS: He won't listen to us.

**VINCE:** He doesn't care.

**RANEM:** We can go on TV.

**CHRIS:** Great idea! A special bulletin has just come in:

> *SAMANTHA makes a bomb sound, dropping the bulletin into CHRIS's hand.*

A large gang of angry school kids have been seen protesting. They are considered to be dangerous . . . and armed.

> *They all wave their arms.*

**VINCE:** And legged!

> *VINCE waves his legs.*

. . . But we could . . . we really could.

**CHRIS:** Well, why not? Why shouldn't we? We don't have to be invisible.

**GEORGIE:** Right.

**CHRIS:** And we won't go on the trip because we'll be too busy making petitions.

**VINCE:** Yes!

CHRIS: I can go to Krystal Park any old time. But if Ranem can't go, I won't go!

GEORGIE: Me too!

RANEM: You sure?

CHRIS: Sure we're sure.

VINCE: Yeah.

GEORGIE: Yeah.

CHRIS: Yeah.

> *They all look at* SAMANTHA. *She looks away. Slight pause. Blackout. Music.*

# SCENE FOUR

*The lights come up to a half-light. GEORGIE and VINCE enter, working on the petitions. The lights fade up to full and the music fades out.*

GEORGIE: Oh, no!

VINCE: What is it?

GEORGIE: This is the twenty-fifth petition I've prepared to be signed.

VINCE: Good.

GEORGIE: But I think I spelled the president's name wrong.

*VINCE looks at it sideways and upside down.*

VINCE: I think you're right. It's wrong.

GEORGIE: Now I have to do all of these over again.

VINCE: I'll help you.

**GEORGIE:** Thanks.

*CHRIS and RANEM enter.*

**CHRIS:** Got any more petitions ready? Look at all the ones filled out so far.

**VINCE:** Two hundred names.

**GEORGIE:** Any doubles?

**CHRIS:** Doubles?

**GEORGIE:** People who have signed twice. Or three times. Or four times.

**CHRIS:** Ah, no. Nobody's signed these four times.

**GEORGIE:** Let me look . . . Christopher, this page is all your signature. You signed it thirty-five times. Christopher Welch, Christopher Welch, Christopher Welch.

**CHRIS:** I was only trying to help.

**GEORGIE:** Well, you're not.

**CHRIS:** So I made a mistake.

**GEORGIE:** A big one.

*GEORGIE tears up the paper.*

**CHRIS:** Wait! Don't!

**GEORGIE:** It's not good for anything.

**CHRIS:** I was going to give it to my mom. I've never signed my name that many times in a row before. I thought she might like to put it on the fridge.

*GEORGIE gives him the torn pieces of paper.*

**GEORGIE:** Get some Scotch tape and it'll be as good as new . . . and don't do it again.

**CHRIS:** All right.

**VINCE:** We told Mr. Thomas why we weren't going on the trip.

**RANEM:** Was he unhappy with us?

**VINCE:** No, he understood. He said he respected us, said it showed we were serious. In fact, the school is going to postpone all school trips until further notice. And he signed the petition.

*SAMANTHA enters.*

**GEORGIE:** But she's still going.

**SAMANTHA:** My dad's taking me for my birthday. Just because you aren't going doesn't mean I can't.

CHRIS: But you should help us. What's happening to Ranem isn't fair.

SAMANTHA: I know it's not fair—but why should I suffer too?

VINCE: Because next time it could be youuuu!

SAMANTHA: But I want to go to Krystal Park.

RANEM: Everybody does.

SAMANTHA: Well, you can do what you want. I want to go on that Devil Mountain roller coaster. I want to wear my neon shirt and pants and jacket.

CHRIS: It's still not fair.

SAMANTHA: I don't care. I won't miss it. I'm going to go. I'm going.

*Slight pause. SAMANTHA exits.*

CHRIS: The creep.

GEORGIE: I don't blame her.

CHRIS: What? You don't blame her?

GEORGIE: No. It is her birthday. If I were in her shoes, I'd probably go too.

VINCE: Really?

GEORGIE: Yeah. I want to go. I'm dying to go to Krystal Park and go on rides all day and eat caramel popcorn. I mean, look at you guys. You just want a chance to yell about something. And all Vince cares about is getting a stupid BMX anyway. You don't care about going.

CHRIS: That's not true. I want to go.

GEORGIE: Then go. Don't let me stop you.

CHRIS: But I'm not going.

GEORGIE: Well you should. Go home and tell your moms and dads to take you.

CHRIS: What's with her?

RANEM: She is sad. She wants to go on the trip.

GEORGIE: Why do we have to fight for our rights all the time? They don't care. Neither did that man who put his dog on you, Vince. All they know is that we're a different colour than them and they don't like us.

CHRIS: I'm a different colour than you and I like you.

GEORGIE: Thanks, but what about the rest of them?

CHRIS: We'll keep working like this with the petitions and other stuff. Maybe they'll change.

GEORGIE: *(cynically)* Maybe.

VINCE: Maybe.

RANEM: Maybe.

VINCE: If I only had a BMX. I'd take the petitions and deliver them on my bike right to the CBC.

GEORGIE: Your dad wouldn't let you ride it there.

VINCE: Of course he would. For something like this.

CHRIS: But you're never gonna get a BMX, so why worry about it?

VINCE: I could. I might.

GEORGIE: He's right. Why worry about it. We can't do anything. And first thing in the morning, Samantha gets to go to Krystal Park all dressed up in her neon clothes.

CHRIS: She'll have so much neon stuff on she'll turn radioactive.

VINCE: Let's get some more petitions signed.

RANEM: Good idea.

CHRIS: Come on, Georgie. There's lots to do.

GEORGIE: Okay . . . Dear Prime Minister, Dear President . . .

> CHRIS *looks at the petitions. He picks up a pen and looks furtively around.*

CHRIS: I'll just sign a few more . . .

*Blackout. Music.*

## SCENE FIVE

*Lights fade up to a half-light. RANEM, GEORGIE, and CHRIS are counting petitions. The lights come up full and the music fades out.*

**RANEM:** . . . Five hundred seven . . . five hundred eight . . .

**CHRIS:** Five hundred and eight. That's amazing. We got five hundred and eight people to sign these things. That is very impressive. I am impressed.

**GEORGIE:** Yeah, so? Nothing is going to happen. The government won't do anything and Samantha will be back any minute all glowing from Krystal Park and all we did was waste our time.

**CHRIS:** We're not wasting our time. Something might happen.

**GEORGIE:** What? This stuff won't get past the secretaries. It'll go straight in the rubbish bin and then you'll have nothing.

**RANEM:** Not so. I gave these to Mr. Thomas. He made copies of all the petitions. Now we have three copies, see? All in envelopes. Look at the addresses.

**GEORGIE:** *(reading)* The Prime Minister, House of Commons, Ottawa . . . The President of the United States . . . What's the other one say? To the *News Hour* . . . Maybe they will do something.

**CHRIS:** Where's Vince? I thought he wanted to deliver this stuff.

**GEORGIE:** Waiting for his BMX, I guess.

**CHRIS:** Poor sucker. He'll never get one. Let's chip in for his bus fare . . . Here's a dime.

**RANEM:** Here's some . . .

> SAMANTHA *enters. She is wearing her neon clothes.*

**GEORGIE:** Well, look who's back—the world traveller.

**CHRIS:** My sunglasses, my sunglasses, you're blinding me!

**RANEM:** Hi.

**GEORGIE:** How was the trip?

**SAMANTHA:** Do you really want to know?

**CHRIS:** Did you go on Devil Mountain?

**SAMANTHA:** Course.

**GEORGIE:** Well, tell us what happened, it's the least you can do.

SAMANTHA: We drove there. And then we came back. That's all. We went to some shops. Ate pizza and candy and chocolate and drank Coke.

CHRIS: Chocolate?

SAMANTHA: Yeah. Here, I brought you some back.

CHRIS: Thanks!

*CHRIS grabs the candy and starts to eat, then notices the others eyeing him. He sheepishly passes the bag around.*

GEORGIE: *(to SAMANTHA)* Any trouble crossing the border?

SAMANTHA: Just the usual. They talked to my father for a long time, searched the car, looked over our passports. And sent us on our way.

CHRIS: They searched your car? Cool! That never happens to us!

*The others give him blistering looks.*

What? Has that happened to you?

GEORGIE: Every time.

CHRIS: Why?

*He sees their glowering faces.*

Oh.

GEORGIE: So what happened when you got there?

SAMANTHA: It was raining. I got soaked. So we ducked inside a gift shop. My dad bought me a little key ring with Devil Mountain on it.

VINCE: Let's see!

*SAMANTHA glumly holds it out. Everybody admires it.*

RANEM: Did you go into the science fair?

SAMANTHA: It was in a big building. Hundreds of projects. None of them were as good as your kite.

VINCE: You would have won for sure!

RANEM: Not this time, maybe next.

CHRIS: What about Devil Mountain!

SAMANTHA: My dad suggested that first we warm up on the Ferris wheel and bumper cars.

VINCE: I love bumper cars!

SAMANTHA: I hate getting bumped. And I was still soaking wet—I was freezing. So I ate more chocolates to warm myself up.

CHRIS: You have any more of those?

SAMANTHA: Here. Take it all.

CHRIS: Thanks!

*CHRIS gorges on the chocolates.*

GEORGIE: And then what happened?

SAMANTHA: Nothing.

CHRIS: So did you go on Devil Mountain?

SAMANTHA: Uh-huh.

CHRIS: How many times did you go? Six? Seven?

SAMANTHA: . . . Once.

CHRIS: Just once?

GEORGIE: Once?

RANEM: Once?

SAMANTHA: I got on it and was so excited I couldn't wait to get on top and glow. There were three loops, four loops, I couldn't wait. Some kids were afraid to go but I wasn't. I had enough money for ten rides. Finally it started, kind of slow at first as it goes up the mountain and up to the top of the first loop and then it goes screaming down.

CHRIS: Was it great?

SAMANTHA: I don't know. I felt sort of funny.

CHRIS: *(eating a chocolate)* Why?

SAMANTHA: I was too excited to eat all day except for those chocolates. I could really feel them in my stomach.

CHRIS: The chocolate?

SAMANTHA: Yeah, the chocolate.

CHRIS: Oh.

SAMANTHA: Then we started going up the second loop. I could see everybody way down below and the seagulls were flying around my head . . .

RANEM: Nice.

SAMANTHA: I started feeling dizzy. I started turning green. And then at the top of the loop . . .

CHRIS: What?

SAMANTHA: *(whispering)* . . . I threw up.

CHRIS: Ohhhhh . . .

SAMANTHA: I don't know how I finished the ride. I thought I was going to die. I thought I was dead. I've never been so sick in my whole life.

GEORGIE: Still, it was fun to go and everything.

SAMANTHA: I don't remember. I was too sick.

RANEM: Happy birthday.

SAMANTHA: Thanks . . . I should have stayed home. Stayed with you guys . . . I'm sorry, Ranem. You should have been at the science fair. You really would have won.

RANEM: There will be other chances. Scientific knowledge must never disappear.

GEORGIE: Besides, I'm glad you went. At least we know what we missed.

CHRIS: Oh, gag. I never want to eat chocolate again.

*VINCE enters. He is wearing a BMX jacket.*

VINCE: Hi.

ALL: Hi, Vince.

VINCE: I'm ready to take the petitions to the post office and the news.

CHRIS: Good. We've put together the bus fare for you.

VINCE: I don't need it.

CHRIS: What, planning to walk?

VINCE: No. I went home last night and my mom and dad were standing there and they had this funny look on their faces. I didn't know what was up. Then my dad says to me, "I got a riddle for you: What's got an alloy stem, full chrome plating, and chromoly frame and forks?" I said, "Only one thing's got an alloy stem, full chrome plating, and chromoly frame and forks." So he said, "Next Christmas, all you get is a stocking, and on your birthday all you get is a cake." And I said, "Why?" And he said, "Because all your presents are right here now." And there it was.

*The lights change into magical colours. The* Star Wars *theme plays. Slowly, incredibly, a glowing BMX appears, perhaps from the sky.*

My own bike. My own BMX.

*It touches the ground. He sits on it.*

It's beautiful. It's mine.

*He wheels it around, performs a few stunts.*

I can do wheelies and bronkies and table tops. My bike! My BMX!

*The lights return to normal. The kids are in awe.*

CHRIS: Can I ride it? Can I ride it!

VINCE: First ride is for the person who is delivering the petitions.

SAMANTHA: Who?

*VINCE goes to GEORGIE and puts a helmet on her. She shakes hands all around.*

**CHRIS:** Here are the petitions. This one is for the post office, special delivery to Ottawa, and this one goes straight to the CBC. Good luck.

*GEORGIE joins VINCE on the bike. He adjusts his visor. She taps him on the helmet.*

**RANEM:** Wait! Take this with you!

*He hands GEORGIE his kite. The others cheer and wave goodbye as the kite flies behind them.*

He got his BMX.

**CHRIS:** I don't believe it.

**SAMANTHA:** Do you think it'll work?

**CHRIS:** You mean the president, will he do anything?

**RANEM:** Maybe. Maybe not.

**CHRIS:** At least we're doing something.

**SAMANTHA:** Right.

*SAMANTHA reaches into her pocket.*

Oh, Christopher, do have some more chocolate.

**CHRIS:** Aaaaaaaaaaaargh.

*Beat. The kids turn as if they're watching TV, listening to news anchors' voices.*

**NEWS 1:** A group of sixth graders are in the news today . . .

**NEWS 2:** Over one thousand signatures protesting the border restrictions . . .

**NEWS 3:** Young scientist, Ranem Al Shiakh, prevented from attending an international science fair . . .

**NEWS 1:** Mr. President: What are you going to do about it? More news at nine.

*The kids cheer. Blackout. Music: Bob Marley's "One Love."*

Dennis is the co-founder of Vancouver's acclaimed Green Thumb Theatre and served as artistic director for twelve years. As a playwright, his body of plays continues to be produced internationally in numerous languages. Dennis has received the British Theatre Award, two Chalmers Canadian Play Awards, the Jesse Richardson Career Achievement Award, and the International Arts for Young Audiences Award. He's won a Gemini, two WGC Awards, three Leos, and a Robert W. Wagner Award for his screenplays. Dennis wrote the screenplay for the feature film *Life Above All*, Prix François Chalais winner at the 2010 Cannes Film Festival, 2011 Academy Award Shortlist for Best Foreign Language Film, and a Leo winner for Best Screenplay.

Originally published by Pulp Press, 1989.
First Playwrights Canada Press edition: September 2006. Second
edition: November 2018.
Printed and bound in Canada by Rapido Books, Montreal

Cover design by Christine Mangosing // CMANGO Design

Playwrights Canada Press
202-269 Richmond St. W.
Toronto, ON
M5V 1X1

416.703.0013
info@playwrightscanada.com
www.playwrightscanada.com